D1209636

IRONDOC

PRACTICAL
STRESS MANAGEMENT TOOLS
FOR PHYSICIANS

Mamta Gautam, MD, FRCPC, MOT

IRONDOC
Practical Stress Management Tools for Physicians
Mamta Gautam, MD, FRCPC, MOT

Copyright © 2004
Mamta Gautam
Suite 512, 11 Holland Avenue
Ottawa, Ontario. Canada K1Y 4S1
(613) 729-3794
www.drgautam.com

Published by:
Book Coach Press, Ottawa, ON, Canada
www.BookCoachPress.com
info@BookCoachPress.com

Cover and graphic design: Donald Lanouette
Editing: Serena Williamson and Leslie Rubec

Printed in Canada

Library and Archives Canada Cataloguing in Publication
Gautam, Mamta, 1961-
Irondoc: practical stress management tools for
physicians/Mamta Gautam, 1ST Ed.
Includes bibliographical references.
ISBN: O-9735207-4-4

1. Physicians-Pyschology 2. Physicians-Job Stress
1. Physicians-Mental health 2. Stress management I. Title.

RC455.4.S87G37 2004   155.9'042'08861   C2004-905734-0

For

Mark, Nik, Shaun, and Neal

Thanks for filling my life with

love and laughter.

CONTENTS

CHAPTER 5

CHAPTER 6

CHAPTER 7

ABOUT THE AUTHOR

Mamta Gautam, MD, FRCPC is a psychiatrist in private practice in Ottawa, and an Assistant Professor in the Department of Psychiatry, University of Ottawa. She is a specialist in Physician Health and Well-being. Hailed as "The Doctor's Doctor"; physicians have made up her entire patient population for the past decade.

Dr. Gautam is the first Director of the University of Ottawa Faculty Wellness Program, an innovative and comprehensive physician wellness program, which is the first of its kind at any academic setting in the world. This program served as the template for CMA Centre for Physician Health and Well-being, where she serves as the Chair of the Expert Advisory Group. She is Co-Chair of the Canadian Psychiatric Association Section on Physician Health. She writes a regular column, Helping Hand, in the *Medical Post*, on Physician Health.

Dr. Gautam is an internationally known expert and speaker. She has given over 400 keynote presentations and workshops in the area of physician stress and mental health, work-life balance in medicine, communications, and conflict resolution skills. She has created videos, and authored numerous articles and book chapters on this topic. She is on the faculty of several Physician Leadership Conferences throughout Canada and the United States. She is the President Elect of the Ontario Psychiatric Association.

ACKNOWLEDGEMENTS

First and foremost, I would like to gratefully acknowledge all of my physician colleagues who trusted me, and gave me the privilege of caring for them. Without them, I would have never gained the interest or expertise that has led me to this point.

My editor, Serena Williamson, has been invaluable in bringing this concept to fruition. Her enthusiasm and hard work, under tight deadlines, have helped keep me focused and productive. I am grateful for Donald Lanouette's creative genius and his ability to bring my ideas to life on the cover.

There are many people in my life who have served as supporters and promoters of my work and me, and I would like to thank them. I am not able to acknowledge everyone by name; there are so many people who have been on this journey with me. There are many people who have asked me to speak to their group, who have organized and planned the conferences, and the attentive colleagues and spouses in the audience, to all of whom I owe a thanks.

Thank you to my dear friend, Dr. Susan Swiggum, who started me on this path, in her year as President of the Federation of the Medical Women of Canada, and asked me to give that talk on depression which was the turning point and led to my first three physician-patients. She has continued to promote my work at the many organizations in which she has been involved.

Thank you to Drs. Alan Buchanan and Tony Sehon, Psychiatric Update for Family Physicians, friends and mentors, who took a chance on me and asked me to present at their conferences. In particular, thank you, Alan, for taking the time after my first presentation, to sit with me, go through each slide, tear apart the entire thing, reduce me to tears, and tell me that it was for my own good because I was "good but could be great." I have looked back on that hour many times, often before new presentations, each time with greater appreciation of what you did for me. Also, thanks for the talk on the beach in the Caribbean, where the idea of this book all began.

Thank you to Dr. Michael Myers, who is a pioneer in the field of Physician Health, and has become an invaluable mentor and a cherished friend. His wisdom, expertise and advice have helped me through many years of this work. There is a small but growing group of us like-minded physicians, dedicated to the care of colleagues. I am indebted to, and inspired by, them all.

My PALS journal club members have been a constant source of support, and ongoing reassurance, encouragement and affirmation. We have all grown during the past ten years together, and they provide my safe place where I can ask stupid questions and get intelligent answers.

My personal friends are a key part of how I manage my stress. Their ongoing support on regular weekends away biking, cooking, wine-tasting and skiing help preserve my sanity. You know who you are; I shall constantly remind you.

My family – my mother, Rama, who is the most courageous woman I know; and my four sisters, Rita, Vinita, Alka, and Monica – have always been there to offer guidance and love. Our sisters' weekend away is a highlight of each year. Imagine – the five Gautam Girls set loose in a city near you! A special thank you to Monica, who sat with me at the computer and typed each word of my very first handout; helped me learn PowerPoint for my very first presentation; and essentially convinced me that the computer would not blow up if I pressed the wrong key! My in-laws Norma and Llewellyn are an integral part of my family, and are always available to offer help, support, and apple pie.

My husband, Mark, and my three sons, Nik, Shaun and Neal, are the four legs on which my life is solidly balanced. Thank you for giving me the time and space to write these thoughts. Thank you for sharing me with my colleagues. Thank you for your constant love and laughter.

INTRODUCTION

This book has been in my head for several years. Working with physicians for the past decade, I have seen how we all share similar patterns of thought and behaviour that lead both to our successes and our stresses. Physicians have a dream — of being the perfect doctor, saving lives, curing illness, stamping out disease. As their careers progress, with the inevitable imposition of the limitations of reality, the dream continues, requiring increasingly greater effort to maintain. This dream encompasses their private lives, too, with physicians also striving to be the perfect partners and the perfect parents. Physicians try to be all things to all people. In doing so, their personal needs are last, and often lost. Thus is laid the foundation for stress in medicine.

Physician stress is a fact. It can be positive, enriching and motivating. When it becomes negative and hurtful, it becomes a problem. It is this negative stress that I hope to address in this book.

The initials after my name on the cover summarize the qualifications that I bring to this project on Physician Stress. The MD confirms that I am a physician. The FRCPC reassures you that I am a specialist, in Psychiatry, and a fellow of good standing with the Royal College of Physicians and Surgeons of Canada.

The MOT stands for Mother of Three! This is really where I learned about stress and its management. I gave birth to a set of twins when my first son was just a year old, and these three boys have taught me most of what I know about stress, and am going to share with you. In fact, since I have spent more time with them than in my formal specialty training, I decided to award myself the extra initials. I am thrilled to see some of my colleagues using similar designations.

I landed in the field of Physician Health by serendipity. I am a Child Psychiatrist by training. However, when the twins arrived in my final year of fellowship, I decided to restrict my work to clinical practice so I could be more available to the children. A close friend, who was the President of the Federation of Medical Women of Canada that year, asked me to give a talk at the Annual Meeting. The topic was Depression. At the end of this presentation, three of the women in the audience came up to me, told me that I could have been talking about their experience, that I was not as weird as they thought psychiatrists could be, and asked me if I would see them as patients. These were my first three physician patients. Since then, through word of mouth, my clinical practice is now entirely focused on the care of colleagues.

During the past decade, I have been privileged to share the lives of many physician colleagues, and witness and understand their stress. It soon became clear to me that they shared many common characteristics that others outside of my office might be experiencing as well. This knowledge formed the basis of the presentations that I have given over the past ten years on this topic. After many of my talks, I am approached and asked whether I have written a book to reinforce my points. Thanks to all of you who made this suggestion and encouraged this project.

This book is the answer to your requests.

I offer you an innovative concept, the Irondoc, which has translated into a clinically proven strategy for success for physicians. The Irondoc is a concept that allows and promotes balance in medicine. Derived from the Ironman triathlon, it gives physicians permission to succeed by doing their overall best in multiple areas of their life, without having to be the best in each area. This book validates the stress that physicians feel, explores the many causes of this stress, and provides an understanding of the psychology of the physician, which predisposes them to stress. This book then offers tested strategies for dealing with stress, richly illustrated with firsthand case studies and anecdotes. All physicians will recognize themselves among its pages.

This book is intended to be a simple guide to healthier living, not a medical textbook. It will help you recognize that all physicians are vulnerable to stress, that you are not alone if you feel this way, and feel hopeful that there are solutions. It is not intended to be an authoritative source of information on stress, since that information is part of our medical training, and is available to us in other resources. I have purposefully left out the scientific jargon and the medical lingo. Much of this information is common sense and common knowledge. Over the years, I have tried to gather and process this information to make it useful, not to take personal credit for it. All attempts have been made to properly credit sources of unique and specific information.

My goal is to pull together this information in a simple and practical way, so it can be used productively. In his book *Good to Great*, Jim Collins states, "the essence of profound insight is simplicity," and promotes a "piercing insight that allows us to see through complexity and discern underlying patterns… see what is essential, and ignore the rest."

The focus on practicality is what makes this book work. The reader can put the tools it provides into practice the minute the book is opened up. The combination of giving physicians the intellectual awareness of their behaviour patterns, validating their situation with actual vignettes, and then providing them with practical techniques and examples of how they can be used is a winning one. This is not rocket science. However, our ability to intellectualize things makes us feel that we know and have addressed the situation, when, in fact, we have not. This book provides the actual practical steps and strategies to assist us in following through to improve our situation, and manage our stress. It will help you stay the course in medicine and emerge victorious.

I recall a wedding shower gift from years ago that stands out among all the thoughtful and stunning gifts of silver, crystal and linen received — a shiny red toolbox, practical and sturdy, filled with all the basic tools we could ever need. This gift has stood the test of time, has always been handy and available when needed, and has proven to be the most practical and reassuring gift of all. Like the toolbox, this book has been filled, with care, with a wide variety of strategies detailed to help physicians better manage their stress. These are easy to learn, and proven to work. These tools remain in the toolbox, ready and available for use when needed. It is my hope that this book will be your shiny red toolbox, my similarly practical, useful, reassuring gift to you.

CHAPTER 1

ON YOUR OWN COUCH

There it is. Again. That little voice in the back of your head that you have been avoiding, that has been telling you things are not quite right. Today, you're exhausted, and can't even summon up the energy to find something else to do, to keep busy so you won't have to think about it.

As you look back, you can see that it has been coming on for some time. Sure, you have been doing fine at work. You managed to meet all of your responsibilities there. The patients are well cared for, the paperwork is completed, and you are getting to most of the meetings. You even make time to check and answer your emails, glance through the journals and surf your favourite sites on the Internet. However, at the end of the workday, you have little left to give. You really need a break and just want to be left alone.

In the past few months, there has been a difference. You realize that you are not enjoying your work as much as you used to do. You have been more negative and cynical, and more easily frustrated. You are feeling more irritable with staff, colleagues and patients. The paperwork has not been completed in your usual efficient way. You push through the day, but at the end of it, you're done.

Trying to handle what others want from you is too much, and you start to avoid people. At work, you get too busy to attend meetings, and start grabbing a coffee or sandwich at your desk, instead of going to the cafeteria or coffee shop. After work, you're now sneaking into your own house, so you can get a few minutes to yourself before anyone realizes you are home. You hide behind the newspaper or at the computer, hoping they will not interrupt you. You find ways to get out of social functions, not return phone calls from friends, and stay at home alone. Actually, this has not been so hard to do, because you have not been well. You have had more colds this year than in the past decade combined; they have lasted much longer than before. The migraines are occurring more frequently, and more intensely.

Today is one such day. You snapped at your nurse because a patient's lab test results were not back yet and on the file. The patients all seemed to demand and complain more than usual. You were considering pinning to the front of your lab coat a huge button that shouted "WHAT DO YOU WANT FROM ME?" The migraine started, predictably, by noon. At the end of the afternoon, you were running late, and the charts had piled up. You glanced at them once, felt overwhelmed, and left for home.

Here you are now, lying alone on the couch. The big annual barbecue with your medical school friends is tonight, and your family had waited for you to get home so that you could all attend together. It was bad enough that you were late; your critical and sarcastic comments about the friends were finally too much, and they all stormed out ahead of you. You are too exhausted to even turn on the television and tune things out.

Your thoughts surge forward unchecked. What's wrong with me? Where did the fun in life go? Am I burning out?

Am I depressed? You haven't been yourself for months now. At that moment, you decide that you don't want to feel like this anymore. You think about going for help.

Going for help? Great — out of the frying pan into the fire! More thoughts... *That's just for patients; I'm a doctor, not a patient. People will think I am weak, a failure. I will be really embarrassed; no one can know about it. How will I find time to see a doctor? I don't have enough time to do all the things I have on my plate now. This may mean that I can't get medical insurance anymore. I don't want this on my record. Perhaps I can just try harder, do the things that I advise my own patients to do. What if people find out, and stop referring patients to me, and my practice shuts down? Where do I go for help?*

Perhaps I could just try myself on some medication first. The sample cupboard is full of antidepressants. The patients do well with them, and seem to tolerate them well. That way, no one would know or find out, and I would just feel better. No, that's not right; I can't be my own doctor. I should get some help.

I can't do it. Yet, I can't NOT do it. Enough is enough!

You get up, and look for the list of resources you have somewhere. Actually it is not so hard to find, since you had been looking at it almost daily lately. You push yourself to make the phone call, and leave a message. It feels good to actually say that you are not doing well and want some help. Relieved, you drop back on the couch. You have taken the first, hardest, step.

CHAPTER 2

ANTICIPATING THE OTHER COUCH

You can't believe that you are actually here, in the waiting room, waiting to see the therapist. It has been months coming, allowing you the time to admit you are not well, and to acknowledge that you need some help to feel better. Thinking back to the phone call you made, you are so grateful that you got a return call the next day. It made it easier to not back down. You had no time for the usual pep talk that you had always used to convince yourself that it is not so bad, no time to put up the usual barriers that had prevented you from seeking help before, and stay stuck. You had let it go for too long; luckily the therapist understood that, and she made arrangements to see you quickly.

Then, you start to worry about what to say. What is she expecting? Should I have this all written out, like a case presentation? Perhaps I have some of the dates wrong? You wait and hope it goes fine. You really have nothing to lose. You have done all that you can by yourself.

It is hard to be the patient. As doctors, we are care givers, not care receivers. We are not comfortable receiving care from others. This is not the role that we were trained to do. We also like to be in control. Letting someone else take over the control is not easy to do.

IRONDOC

The door opens and the therapist comes out to greet you. You have made it this far. It will get better.

CHAPTER 3

ON THE OTHER COUCH

When I work with my patients, the initial assessment is usually a question-and-answer situation. Although later sessions are more unstructured, at first it is important to review all that has happened. Together, we identify how you have been feeling, and what signs and symptoms you have been experiencing recently. We acknowledge the stressors in your life, both professionally and personally. We explore whether this has happened before, and whether any of your family members have struggled with similar difficulties. We define preexisting medical illnesses, and medications being used that may be contributing to the current situation.

You learn that, as a doctor, you are under stress regularly. You learn how to distinguish what is normal, and what is not healthy.

Having acknowledged that stress is an inherent part of medicine, let's focus on understanding how and why it can happen. In psychiatry, we use a biopsychosocial approach to formulate an understanding of a situation. Let's apply that same approach here, to understand why we feel such stress in medicine. We will start with the biological and social demands first, and then add the psychological aspects in the following chapter.

Biological Factors

The biological factors that predispose physicians to stress are many and varied. These include the following conditions.

Lack of sleep: This is the number one complaint among physicians. The long hours of work, being on call at night, and frequent nights on call prevent us from getting the necessary amount of sleep that allows our bodies to function normally. Experts agree that we all require at least 8-10 hours of sleep each night. Physicians average 2-4 hours of sleep during a night on call. On a semi-regular basis, this depletes our reserves and prevents our bodies' ideal responses in all situations.

Poor Eating Habits: Good nutrition is a key aspect in maintaining a healthy body. Too often, the physician is too busy to eat regular, well-balanced meals. Meals are either skipped, or hastily put together. Fast foods from the hospital cafeteria, coffee shop or vending machines are quickly consumed. Extra meals are added on while awake during long, busy nights.

Poor Level of Fitness: We have less time for fitness, for ourselves. We are too busy with someone or something more urgent, and often mean to get to it later. But later, we are too tired, and anticipating another busy day tomorrow, we choose to rest instead.

These three lifestyle factors affect our bodies constantly. Our busy lives often prevent us from providing ourselves with these very basic needs.

Positive Family History of Psychiatric Illness: Some of us are genetically predisposed to psychiatric illness. Having a first degree relative with a psychiatric illness greatly increases our chances of having similar difficulties. This lowers our levels of tolerance to stress, and minimizes our skills in coping with this stress.

Overuse of Drugs and Alcohol: There is controversy among experts regarding whether physicians overuse drugs and alcohol more than others in the general population. Even if substance abuse is not more prevalent in medicine, it remains a more serious problem. For those among us who are more vulnerable to this behaviour, it becomes more serious because we have relatively more money to spend on drugs or alcohol; we have greater access to drugs (medication samples in the office, medications available in the hospital, or writing our own prescriptions); and the drugs we can access are more serious. At least one third of all hospitalizations of physicians are related to drug dependency. Every physician knows a physician that has a problem of impairment. The good news is that early intervention with physician alcoholics results in an 80% success rate!

Psychiatric Illness: Anxiety Disorders and Depression, as well as Adjustment Disorders with anxious or depressed mood, are the most common diagnoses of physicians treated in the outpatient psychiatry setting. Although depression is reported to be present in one out of every three or four physicians at some point in their life, these figures may reflect underreporting and self-treatment. I recently reviewed the charts of the last 100 physicians referred to me, and discovered that just over 80% of them had already started themselves on an antidepressant medication, without the advice or knowledge of their own family physician. This underreporting occurs because of the physician's reluctance to acknowledge the problems and to go for help. The medication, usually one of the relatively new SSRIs (Selective Serotonin Reuptake Inhibitors), is easily available to the physician-patient; works effectively; has few, if any, side effects; and is well tolerated. This is a serious issue, because depressed physicians need assistance to be treated. Usually, if self-treated, the improvement is either partial or temporary. Physicians have greater incidence of suicide as compared to that of the general population, with the rate in males being 1.5 to 2.0 times that of the general population, and increasing to 3.0 to 4.0 times for female physicians.

Social Demands

Physicians also have to deal with multiple social demands, from several areas of their lives. These fall into four general categories: Career and Work Related Demands; Household Responsibilities; Relationships; and Personal Goals.

1. Career and Work Related Demands

The work of a physician is a key source of many demands that lead to stress.

The Dream of Being a Physician: All physicians have a dream: to be the best doctor ever, to save lives, stamp out illness, eradicate disease. Think back to the first year of medicine — we couldn't wait to be real doctors, to be important, to contribute. We were keen and eager, and took care to look the part, with the crisp white lab coat, the pockets bulging with books, the stethoscope around our neck, and our pager. Imagine, we actually wanted our pagers to go off— then! As our careers progress, we have to deal with the inevitability of our limitations. Not every patient can be saved or cured. Yet, this dream is propagated and reinforced by our teachers and our training. Of course, our patients love this dream too. Giving up and grieving this dream is a major source of the stress of medicine.

Our patients: The majority of our patients are wonderful and enjoyable. Yet, some are demanding, unappreciative, dissatisfied, and make most contact with them stressful. Dealing with patients and their problems constantly requires intense emotional contact, and is draining. There is no way to know precisely what issue or concern they will bring to the session, and we must be prepared and able to deal with it all, deftly shifting gears with each new patient. There is greater demand and expectations as we deal with a well-informed public, with current access to information through the Internet. We all practice under the cloud of a possible lawsuit, or the risk of complaints to our licensing bodies. A complaint or lawsuit is very stressful, leading to anxiety, insecurity and deflation of our confidence.

Occupational Hazards: There are many occupational hazards in the practice of medicine. There is the risk of contracting serious disease and infection, such as AIDS, SARS, hepatitis, or tuberculosis. The threat of violence is a reality for physicians, especially women physicians and physicians working in the fields of Psychiatry and Emergency Medicine. Sexual harassment continues to be an issue, as it is in any other work environment. The lack of sleep can lead to physical exhaustion and possibly impaired judgment.

Medicine as a Business: Running a medical practice is running a business. Yet, few physicians practicing for more than five years were taught anything about business, as a medical student or resident. It is stressful to do things at which we know that we are not particularly good. This lack of knowledge is slowly starting to change for the better, as this gap in our training is being recognized and filled. There is the initial business of setting up a practice, choosing a location, leasing office space, negotiating rents, setting up files and attracting patients. Then we have to run the office, schedule patients, hire and manage staff, bill for services and complete paperwork on time.

Maintenance of Competence: There is a vast amount of new information in medicine, and a need to keep up with this. We need to sift through the huge numbers of journals that find their way onto our desks. We need to attend meetings and conferences regularly to keep abreast of new developments. The requirements for increased medical and technological knowledge have increased, but the time available for this has diminished.

Organizational Changes in Health Care: We are working in a time of major health care reform, and a rapid pace of change of the health care system. There is reduction and redistribution of funds in health care, with no clear ideas on the ultimate outcome.

There is political and economic uncertainty. There are hospital closures and mergers, and often, physicians are not able to have much input into these decisions. As stressful as it is to deal with these changes, the stress is increased by having to work with colleagues who are also feeling the stress. All of us struggle to find resources. As waiting lists for specialist consultation and care increases, family physicians are dealing with patients who are sicker than ever and require more time and input. For some, there is forced retirement. Physicians are feeling a loss of geographic flexibility and independence. As physicians speak out against short-sighted changes to the health care system, there is often a lack of sympathy and understanding of their cause by the media and the public.

Issues Specific to Women: Women in medicine have to deal with the minority status of their gender. Discrimination and scapegoating continue to exist. Female physicians relate stories of being ignored at meetings, of not being listened to or being mocked, of their family commitments being ridiculed, and of their academic contributions being negated. Women work in relative isolation, with few other women physicians to network with, or to serve as mentors. There are rarely women in high positions in academic settings, to serve as role models and to provide encouragement. Add to this the life stage considerations. At the very time that the male colleagues in medicine are gearing up their careers, women are taking time out to have children.

I recall completing my fellowship, pregnant with twins, with a one-year-old at home. As my male peers complained about all the forms to fill out for obtaining a university appointment, I was thinking "Three car seats...Can I fit three car seats in the back of my Honda?"

2. Household Responsibilities

When we finally get home from work, the household responsibilities are still there waiting for us.

Managing the household: This includes activities such as grocery shopping, cooking meals and cleaning the house. Professional women still retain the primary role for this. Some of us feel that we have to do it all, and we can learn to allow ourselves permission to give this responsibility to someone else. Even if the work is delegated, the woman is still often the one responsible for the delegating. It is she who decides what needs to be done, who puts the ad in the paper or contacts the appropriate agency, she who does the phone screening and conducts the interviews, and does the payroll.

Finances: There are additional responsibilities dealing with setting a budget, and making savings and investment decisions. This is a big source of stress, as this is an area in which most physicians have little or no training and experience. There is more pressure to work harder in the face of cutbacks to maintain the same income. Despite diminishing financial resources, our financial commitments such as office expenses or mortgage are often the same or increasing. This may involve changing our expectations of what we had hoped to achieve, with an associated sense of loss. With all the changes pending in the health care system, we are unable to make long-term plans. There remains a lot of anxiety about where we will be in the future.

3. Relationships

The people in our lives are a source of joy, but dealing with them and their needs can often be a source of stress.

Childcare and Eldercare: We are referred to as "The Sandwich Generation," sandwiched between the needs of our aging parents, and those of our children. It requires a lot of time to consider the options and to organize the care. Once again, much of this responsibility falls to the woman, whether she works inside or outside the home. Women are usually the ones to adjust their work schedules when required, and remain the primary caretakers. For most working professionals, it is expected that eldercare will overtake childcare as a key concern in the coming decade. Physicians want to spend quality time with the family, and look forward to coming home to do so. However, the stress of juggling our other many demands prevents us from doing this consistently.

Singlehood: Being single is great if it is by choice. This enables us to be more flexible and independent. However, it sometimes feels lonely, and single physicians report a sense of being less accepted by peers socially. Singlehood is a problem if it is not our preferred status. Some physicians are too busy getting through medical school and residency to be in a serious relationship, and feel they missed out on opportunities. As we get older, the likelihood of finding a partner decreases. These physicians feel a sense of loss and ongoing loneliness.

Marital Issues: Physicians experience more difficulties within their marriages due to a high degree of stress and conflict, but have a lower divorce rate than the general population. The lower divorce rate is not well understood, but may be because they work so hard they can avoid dealing with it, and they remain in denial about their problems; they are embarrassed to seek help; their concern about their social status prevents them from separating; or because they work hard to address and resolve these problems. They may experience a sense of guilt because they are so busy, and often leave the bulk of household duties to their partners.

Frequent problems within the marital relationship include difficulties with communication, conflict resolution, intimacy and sexuality. Women physicians are often burdened, as they feel responsible for dealing with the housework and children also. Husbands of female physicians can feel belittled if they earn less than their spouse. The prevalence of abuse of women physicians within their relationships is high, although numbers are unknown. Physicians in gay and lesbian relationships also experience stress, both from inside and outside the relationship.

Friendships: We often do not have time to devote to our friendships. Luckily, most friends do not require this consistently, and understand the multiple demands on our time and energy. Friends play crucial roles in our lives, and offer love, listening, support and nurturance.

They can become lifelines at times of transition, such as when we change jobs, deal with marital separation and divorce, become empty nesters, or deal with serious illnesses such as undergoing chemotherapy.

Community: Many physicians are very involved in their neighbourhood and community. They are leaders in the school councils; coach their children's sports teams; organize neighbourhood events; help underprivileged groups and are visibly involved in religious and spiritual activities. Their leadership skills are recognized and utilized outside of the medical environment. Again, this adds to their load, and increases the stress they manage.

4. Personal Goals

Many physicians want to set personal goals for themselves. They try to make time to pursue their own interests, and care for themselves. Some of us would like to learn something new, such as a new sport or skill. Sometimes, we want to pursue another skill or talent we have enjoyed in the past, such as music or art. We would like to exercise regularly, get involved in sports, and push ourselves to our best efforts. There are times when we just want to be alone, to curl up with a good book and read, or listen to music and relax.

However, in trying to please others, and being so conscientious and responsible, physicians often feel they have to get everything else done before focusing on themselves. Their own needs are last, and often, lost.

CHAPTER 4

INSIGHTS FROM THE COUCH

Psychological Aspects

One of the most important goals of therapy is to gain insight into who we are, why we get ourselves into stressful situations and stay there, and why we cannot stop doing this. This is the "Psychological" part of the biopsychosocial approach to formulating an understanding of a situation.

We explore the patient's background history, look at what life was like while the patient was growing up, and what it was like to grow up in his or her home. This is just the perception of what happened, not necessarily what did occur. This is never meant to blame or criticize, but to understand that while that situation did occur, perhaps for valid reasons and people did their best, it may still have had a negative impact. The goal is to define this impact, especially on the sense of self, and to reduce its effect in adulthood.

Issues Arising From Past Experiences

It is important to understand that our sense of self arises from our past experiences as a child. We establish this sense of self from conclusions, which we drew as children, based on how we perceived we were treated, compared to others. Remember, this may not have been the reality, but it is our perception of the reality.

Three Basic Assumptions

As children, we were still in the concrete phase of our thinking development. At this stage, we were not yet able to extrapolate and think in an abstract fashion. We drew conclusions from what we saw around us.

The basis of our thinking at this phase is the following three assumptions:

1. "Our parents are always right, and know everything." *I recently attended a best-ball golf tournament with my colleagues. Upon my return home, one of my children asked me how many holes-in-one I had shot, earnestly assuming that I would have done so at every hole!*

2. "Our parents should love us and approve of us, be proud of us and brag about us to everyone." *In kindergarten, my children would bring their artwork from school and automatically tape it up all over the kitchen cupboards, because "we knew that you would want to hang them all up, Mommy."*

3. "We are the centre of the world." *A wonderful illustration of this type of thinking is the following story. One of my sons told me about a time when he was about three years old, and was sent up to his room for a timeout. He was upset and stomped all the way to his room, climbed up on his bed, and stomped some more. As he was jumping on his bed, he looked out the window and saw that a car had stopped outside. He thought his jumping had stopped the car.*

He kept jumping, and watched more cars stop. Over the following years, he would try this each time he was in his room, successfully making cars stop. He told me this story, shortly after he looked out one day, and saw the stop sign outside his window!

Our Personal Historian

With these fixed beliefs, we draw conclusions about ourselves in response to how we feel we are treated. Common to physicians is the sense that when we were children, our parents did not approve of us and think we were great. Of course, they were always right and so must be right to think so; and because we were the centre of the world, it must be our fault. We develop our "Historian," the history of ourselves as a person. The common perception is that "We are not good enough; we do not measure up."

We believe this "history" of us, and spend the rest of our lives unconsciously reinforcing this hypothesis, this sense of inadequacy, by rearranging, editing, distorting and selecting facts to fit this theory. When we come across information that does not fit this perception, we omit and negate it. Thus, we perpetuate our need for approval, and our inability to accept approval when we get it. We continue to try to measure up, to be responsible, conscientious, and perfect, and yet retain our chronic self-doubts. These become fixed patterns of behaviour.

How does this occur in a family? Some among us come from families where there was some dysfunction that prevented the parents from being available to meet the needs of the child —

emotional, physical, and/or sexual abuse; alcoholism; absent parent; chronic mental or physical illness in the parent. Parents may have been critical or belittling, or unable to give the positive reinforcement we required. This is harder to understand in other families that did not exhibit obvious dysfunction. In these cases, it is important to gain insight into the dynamics of the family, and how approval was or was not given.

In some cultures, children are encouraged to do their best, and motivated by constantly being reminded of what more they can achieve. Many of us can relate to coming home with 98% on a test, and being asked what happened to the other two marks! It may be meant to motivate, but stated constantly, it helps the child feel that he or she did not measure up. In other families, the performance is taken for granted, and the child is never told that the performance is recognized. Thus, sometimes, it is what happened that is crucial (the abuse, the criticisms); in other situations, it is what did not happen (the lack of recognition and positive feedback) that forms the History.

The History is the Ultimate Distortion. It is created by our internal Historian at a time when we think very concretely, and in this regard only, this concrete thinking persists. The cognition distortions we make as adults, are holdovers of this childlike way of thinking about ourselves. While it is normal thinking for children, it is a distortion for an adult. With psychotherapy, one can learn to identify this distortion, balance it, and "rewrite history."

The 90:10 Rule

This leads to my 90:10 Rule. In any specific situation, only 10 percent of your reaction is due to that particular situation. Ninety percent of the reaction is because of your Historian, what you automatically assumed from your past experiences. Even if you do not fully explore the 90 percent at that time, knowing about it and putting it away, helps you to tone down your reaction at the moment, and deal more appropriately with one-tenth of the feelings.

I recall one winter when my husband, an expert skier, suggested that the family go away for a ski holiday that year. He stated that the children were old enough to start lessons, and that I, too, could take lessons. I was very upset, and proceeded to have one of our biggest fights to date. Then, I recalled the 90:10 Rule; and realized that I was feeling that my husband was saying that, even though I was a good wife, a good mother, a good physician, I was not good enough because I did not ski. I was able to see that this was not at all what he was saying, calm down to a tenth of my initial reaction, and more rationally discuss what to do for our holiday that year.

Common Personality Traits

The Historian helps create some personality traits which, as physicians, we share, and which lead to similar issues and struggles in our lives. The following list of traits is a compilation of the most frequent personality aspects that I see in my office. They are similar to the physician personality described by Gabbard and Menninger (1988.)

Conscientious and Perfectionistic: We constantly strive for perfection. We always need to do more, to be better. We are very conscientious, and do our utmost to meet our responsibilities and attend to all possible details. We try to anticipate others' needs and meet them, often before they are verbalized. This prevents us from relaxing, slowing down, delegating, or feeling that we have done all that we can.

An internist puts in a full day, is exhausted, and calls home to tell his wife he is on his way home. He has signed over to the doctor on call, but decides to make one last visit to his patients on the ward on his way out, just to make sure they're OK. He is at the hospital for a further hour and a half, dealing with the new, but not urgent, concerns that the patients and nurses have.

Marked sense of responsibility: We are very responsible people, and take our responsibilities very seriously. However, we sometimes feel responsible for things that are not under our control. We try to correct things that we see are not right, and feel guilty about things that we cannot fix.

A family physician completes a busy day. At the end of her afternoon, she calls back all the patients she has seen that day, just to make sure that they have completed all the blood tests and X-rays, or filled the prescriptions she had asked of them.

Need for Control: Physicians like to be in control, of ourselves, but also of things and people around us. Sometimes, this is openly and aggressively expressed, but it is equally controlling if done passively, by assumption of the Martyr role. As the martyr, we sacrifice our immediate needs to meet the needs of others. We do not consciously realize that this is actually an attempt to control that others approve of us, and that we are, in fact, meeting our need for approval.

My husband is an Emergency Physician, and he, too, likes to be in control. His need and ability to take control is a real asset to him. As the patient from a car accident is wheeled into his ER, he takes command, instructing the nurses and technicians what to do to assist him. This works in medicine, only because the structure is set up to give the physician this control. He needs to remember that when he walks through our front door at the end of his shift, the children and I do not give him the same control!

People-Pleasing, yet Uncomfortable with Approval Received: The physician tries to please people. We want people to like us. We try to do everything we can for others, but often spread ourselves too thin. We attempt to please everyone, but are left feeling that we have not pleased anyone. When we do get praise or approval from our patients or colleagues, we minimize it and are uncomfortable with it. We dismiss this, and continue to try to win the praise we feel is not ours.

The physician is late at the office daily, accepting patients who call for last-minute appointments. He apologizes when they complain that he is never available, and goes home to complaints because he is late and has missed dinner again. When a patient thanks him the next day, he shrugs it off, saying that it was nothing and that anyone else would have done the same.

Chronic Self-Doubts: Physicians doubt themselves and their abilities, even though others hold them in high regard, feeling they are imposters. We have a fear that, any day soon, people will finally realize how little we know, and our cover will be blown. There is a sense of being lucky so far, of having just managed to pull the wool over others' eyes, of being in the right place at the right time, but of being "found out." This helps to perpetuate the need to be conscientious, responsible, and please people.

A physician is being cited in a lawsuit after a bad outcome for the patient. She knows that she did all that could have been done, documented it all completely, and had multiple consultations as required. But, she cannot stop wondering what more she could have done, what she missed. She is worried that her colleagues will find out and realize that she is not as competent as they thought.

Ability to Delay Gratification/Sense of Entitlement: We are the experts at delaying gratification. We promised ourselves that we would do something, but put it off until…right after we get into medical school, once the exams are over, once we complete the interviews for residency, after this crazy week of call... Yet, when we do feel ready to do something, we want to do it in a big way, because we have waited for it for so long. We often overextend, and get ourselves in trouble. Just because we feel we deserve it, does not mean that we can afford it.

Going through medical school, he watched as his friends settled down to good jobs, got married, bought nice homes. He wanted to wait until after his fellowship exams were over, and he could relax and enjoy himself properly.

When he finished, he and his wife bought a big house in the exclusive area of the city. But, he found himself resentful as he continued to work long hours to pay the mortgage and did not have the time to really enjoy the neighbourhood. When the health care cutbacks occurred, he despaired of ever being able to slow down or retire.

Psychological Defenses

Physicians are intelligent, and therefore, use very highly intellectual defenses, which are psychological mechanisms to protect themselves, unconsciously, from painful emotions. These defenses are important to understand and to identify, because they are major causes for the delay of seeking treatment. Often, physicians seek help when faced with a crisis, such as the death of a patient, family breakup, burnout, acknowledgement of an addiction or a malpractice suit. These defenses make therapy more difficult, as the physician-patient is often saying all the right things that he intellectually realizes may be true, but does not really believe, because he believes the Historian. This gap between what one thinks and what one actually feels is what we refer to as the "Brain-Heart Gap." We attempt to acknowledge and bridge this gap in therapy.

Common intellectual defenses employed include:

Reaction Formation: We form a reaction to our early experiences, and attempt to give the patients and other people in our lives all the attention and approval that we would like to have received.

Denial: We deny that we have any problem. "Patients get sick, not us."

Minimization: We convince ourselves that the problem is much smaller than it really is. "I'm doing all right. I still manage fine at work, don't I?"

Rationalization: We have a reason to explain away the problem. "It's just because I've been on call three times this week; I just need a good night's sleep."

Sublimation: It is crucial to realize that we can use work as a defense, too. We use work to help ourselves feel better, or to distract ourselves from feeling badly. It is useful if we feel depressed because we do not feel we measure up, dissatisfied with our work or home life, or overwhelmed by professional demands. We do what we have always done to feel good about ourselves — just work harder. Sadly, this works because we like what we do, and to do more is fine with us; because there is always more to do and it is satisfying to achieve more; and because the hard-working physician is socially accepted, and even socially admired. Yet, we are just trying to avoid our problems, which eventually do catch up with us.

It becomes easy to see how we have been set up for stress. Physicians dream of being the perfect doctor. As our career progresses, the dream requires increasingly greater effort to maintain. This dream encompasses our private life, too, with physicians also striving to be the perfect partner and the perfect parent.

Physicians try to be all things to all people. We strive to do our ultimate best. In doing so, our personal needs are last, and often lost. Thus is laid the foundation for stress in medicine.

CHAPTER 5

DIAGNOSING THE STRESS

Stress in medicine is a fact. It can be positive, enriching and motivating. When it becomes negative and hurtful, it becomes a problem. Let's address this problem head-on. This is even more necessary in these troubled times of major health care reform and restructuring in the field of medicine.

The Myth in Medicine

The Myth in Medicine is that "We know what we should be doing, therefore, we are doing it." This is simply not true. It is crucial to understand that physicians are not immune to stress. It can happen to any of us.

Five Early Warning Signs of Stress

There are five early warning signs of stress. Under increased stress, you may experience:

1. **Increased physical problems and illnesses:** Under stress, your immune system is not able to function at its optimal level. You are more susceptible to illnesses, such as viral infections, and these occur more frequently and seem to last longer. Preexisting physical problems will be exacerbated, and become more difficult to control using your current regimen.

2. **Increased problems with relationships:** As you become more frustrated and irritable, your usual patience is tested. You are not as easy to get along with. You seem to overreact to situations, and become easily angered. This occurs both at home and at work.

3. **Increased negative thoughts and feelings, about things and people that you previously enjoyed:** It becomes difficult to remember what you saw in them to begin with. You become more critical, and less content.

4. **Increased unhealthy behaviours:** We all have some "bad habits," some things that we know we should not do, but do anyway, rarely. When stressed, these behaviours increase in frequency. Sometimes, it is what we do that is unhealthy – overeating, spending too much, smoking, drinking, gambling. Other times, it is what we stop doing that was good for us – exercising regularly, eating healthily, talking with friends, laughing.

5. **Inability to continue to push ourselves:** We have learned to give up our own needs, and continue to do the right thing. Most physicians function under an amazing amount of stress, and are likely at the threshold much of the time. At this point, we go over the threshold into exhaustion, and cannot keep going as before.

The above five symptoms are signals of serious stress. It is important to watch out for them, in ourselves, and in our colleagues.

Burnout

Stress can lead to burnout. Burnout is a syndrome of chronic overstress. It is not a psychiatric diagnosis, rather a distinct work-related syndrome, occurring when demands exceed resources. Burnout is most likely to occur in jobs that require extensive care-taking, and is common among practicing physicians. There are three stages of burnout, as described by Maslach (1997).

1. **Emotional Exhaustion**
   In this initial stage, people are still able to continue at work, but feel emotionally drained. They go through the paces, and appear to be functioning as normal, but have little or no reserve. The interpersonal interaction is the hardest. For physicians at this stage, we see increasing impatience, frustration and irritability; both at work with patients, staff and colleagues, and at home with partners, children and friends.

2. **Depersonalization**
   At the end of the workday, we have nothing left to give. Since interacting with others is so draining, and we feel exhausted, we start to avoid others, and depersonalize when we are among other people. It seems easier to pull away, than to stay and deal with them.

3. **Decreased Sense of Personal Accomplishment**
   At this advanced stage, physicians no longer enjoy work, find little of the usual satisfaction in dealing with patients and practicing medicine. It becomes hard to remember what it was about medicine that we liked.

Physicians at this stage often think about leaving medicine entirely. Actually, we should reassess and reconsider what we are doing at work about every seven years, and make minor adjustments; such as the numbers of patients we see, the hours that we work, location of the practice, or the focus of our practice. However, this is a healthy, positive, proactive process, unlike the last stage of burnout, which is purely reactive.

A review of studies of burnout in medicine shows high numbers of physicians at each of the stages of burnout. In August 2003, the Canadian Medical Association Physician Resource Questionnaire released results that showed 45.7% of responding physicians were in the advanced stage of burnout. Female physicians were 60% more likely to report burnout, and this may be related to the fact that they felt they were juggling more responsibilities. The likelihood of burnout was shown to increase by 12-15% for each additional hour of work, over 40 hours per week.

Risk factors for burnout include a high workload, with the demands exceeding the available resources. This is a way of life for most physicians. As well, age is shown to be inversely related to burnout. As physicians age, their risk of burnout decreases. This may be because of survivor bias; if they were to experience burnout it would have occurred earlier, and is, therefore, less likely. Also, they may be at a different phase of life, with more time and fewer demands in their personal lives. Having spousal support also helps to minimize emotional exhaustion, and decrease the risk of burnout.

Consequences of Burnout

It is crucial to learn to prevent burnout, or at least to diagnose it in its early stages. Burnout can lead to serious problems, such as impaired job performance, leading to poorer patient care and possible professional problems such as letters of complaint, suspension of hospital privileges and license, or lawsuits. Some physicians end up reducing their work hours, changing jobs within medicine, or leaving medicine entirely. Many physicians experience difficulty with relationships, in both their professional and personal lives. Some experience serious physical problems and illnesses. While burnout is not a psychiatric diagnosis, it can lead to one, contributing to the development of addictions, anxiety disorders, depression and suicide.

So what have we learned so far? We have recognized that stress is normal in medicine, and how we are predisposed to this. We see that it can lead to burnout, which is not normal, and have learned how to recognize the early signs of stress and burnout. Early recognition and response can lead to a positive outcome.

Let's move to the next stage of therapy, where we can use our newfound knowledge to help us prevent stress, and manage it better when it does occur.

CHAPTER 6

BECOMING AN IRONDOC

Balancing our lives in medicine is both a challenge and a necessity. An essential component of success is the skill to attain balance in our lives. The very traits that help us to excel as physicians can also make it difficult for us to achieve this balance easily. We are conscientious, perfectionistic, caring, responsible and people-pleasing. Being like this at work does not leave time and energy for much else.

Balancing Our Work and Home Lives

Balancing the many roles and responsibilities we have is essentially about setting priorities and making choices.

I used to think that balancing my life was easy. I just needed to look at all that I was doing, identify what I liked to do and keep doing that, and identify what I did not like to do and give this up. I soon realized that this was only the first step in the "Balancing Two-Step." The next, harder step was, from the list of all the things that I liked to do, to choose to do some things, and to choose to NOT do some things. Therein lies the challenge: we have to choose to not do things that we like to do, that we are good at doing, which others want us to do. As it has been said, you can do all that you want, just not at the same time!

Juggling Five Balls

As physicians, we are constantly juggling many balls. There is the Work Ball, Relationships Ball, the Home and Family Ball, the Friendships and Community Ball, and the Self-Care Ball. There never seems to be enough time to manage all of these demands as well as we would like. We find ourselves stretched to maintain this juggling act, trying to please everyone and ending up feeling that we have pleased no one. It takes some time to realize that the Work Ball is the only rubber one – drop this one and it will bounce back again and again (even higher than before! Perhaps it is India rubber!) The other ones are more fragile, and easily crack, or even break and shatter, if dropped. So, if you have to let one of these balls drop, make sure it is the Work one.

This juggling act is a dynamic process, a work in progress. There is no perfect way to balance our lives, and what works for one person is different than what would work for another. Also, what works for us at one point in our lives may not work at a later time. All we are required to do is to make a choice that works for us, at this particular phase in life.

Phases

This concept of Phases is a key aspect in the achievement of balance. As we make a choice to let go of something we would have liked to do, it helps to know that this is the best decision for the phase of life we are currently in. When we reach another phase, we may be able to reassess the situation and choose to include what we have had to give up. Life is a series of phases, full of many opportunities for assessment and new choices.

When I had the three babies, I realized that I would not be able to be as academically involved as I had hoped. I chose to limit my work to clinical practice, until the children became older, at which time I would be able to reassess and add on the teaching I had given up earlier. Later, as they were able to stay home alone for short periods, I was at a different phase, and became more involved in administrative work, as I did not have to worry about the children being alone if a meeting went a bit longer than planned.

The Irondoc

Let us become Irondocs. Modeled after the Ironman of the sports world, this is a concept that allows that the physician, although extraordinarily accomplished in multiple areas, need not be the best in any of these areas to be acknowledged as a champion.

The athlete who wins the Ironman Challenge has swam 3.86 km (2.4 miles), biked 180.2 km (112 miles), and ran 42.2 km (26.2 miles) to win this title, and is unquestionably an unparalleled athlete. However, this person is not the best runner in the world, not the best biker in the world, and not the best swimmer in the world. The sports world has recognized this amazing feat, and created a whole new category for such talent, performance and endurance.

I have adapted this to the world of physicians. The term, Irondoc, encourages personal and professional recognition of outstanding achievement in multiple areas of our life, without the impossible demand to be the best in all of those areas. It allows acceptance of our accomplishments as a triumph, and our limitations as an expected reality.

It helps us stay in the race, and complete the course.

This means that we can give ourselves permission to be a good doctor, without having to obtain the largest research grants, or spend the most hours teaching, or keep the cleanest house, or be home with the children all day and bake daily.

In addition, the term exudes a powerful, tough, capable, strong image. We can link this to a series of tools that we can easily acquire and have readily available at our disposal, to manage our stress as physicians. These tools include both basic concepts and specialized strategies outlined in the following chapters.

DEALING WITH STRESS — BASIC TRAINING

We have seen that stress in medicine can come from a variety of sources, and has its origins in biopsychosocial factors.

The Number One Cause of Stress

Regardless of the origin of the stress, it always comes down to one main cause – a sense of lack of control.   In any situation in which we feel stress, it is because we feel a lack of choice, a lack of control. We feel stuck, trapped, with little or no options.

The Number One Solution to Stress

If feeling lack of control is the number one cause of stress, then the number one way to deal with it is to challenge this perception. We need to remember that we actually have more control than we think we have.

Four Steps to Managing Stress

There are four steps to managing stress, and maintaining a sense of control:

1. **Identify the stressor**. Consider what is causing you stress, what the situation is, and write it down. If there are many sources of stress, write them all down. Then, rearrange the list, by identifying which one you would like to address first,

and placing it at the top. Rank the rest of the items on the list similarly. This technique, prioritizing, is helpful. Often, we are so conscientious and perfectionistic that we want to fix it all, immediately, instead being more realistic and productive, and doing this one issue at a time.

2. **Recognize that you have more control than you think you have**. Remember, if thinking that you have no control is what causes stress, then you need to challenge this thought.

3. **Identify what parts of the stressor you can and cannot control**. This is the hardest part of this process. Being intelligent and capable, we approach problems in a logical manner. In most issues that cause us stress, we are only a small part of the situation, perhaps about 2% of the factors. So logically, we focus on the bulk of the problem, the other 98% of the dynamic around us. However, we do not realize that control is an illusion, and that we cannot control anything outside of ourselves. So, we end up trying to control the 98%, of which we have 0% control; and not surprisingly, we feel we have no control. In this process, we forget about our 2% as it feels so relatively minor; however, it is this 2% over which we have 100% control.

4. **Focus on what you can control; learn to cope with what you cannot control**. We need to review what aspects of the situation are our responsibility and under our control. This includes our skills, strengths, weaknesses, knowledge, experience, expectations, hopes, choices, needs, conclusions

and insecurities. Focusing on this helps us reclaim a sense of control in the situation, and banishes the feeling of stress. It gives us the ability to cope with the other 98% in a more productive manner.

The rest of this book will focus on our personal 2%, to reinforce what we can do to remain in control, and manage our stress. This is not meant to convey a sense of helplessness about the other 98%. When we focus on what we can control rather than what we cannot control, it is amazing how our sense of hopelessness is relieved. We feel more powerful, and more in control of the other 98%.

Remember, this sense of lack of control comes from the "Historian." As a child, we are not in control. Compared to the adults, we are younger, physically smaller, have lesser status and are dependent. As adults now, this is no longer true.

Four Questions to Ask

In any situation when you are feeling stress, there are several points to consider, focusing on your personal 2%.

1. **How am I feeling?** Remember, every feeling you have is OK; it is what you do about it that makes it questionable. It is important to allow yourself the feelings and validate them. Instead, most physicians use intellectual defenses. They deny, minimize or rationalize – and so, dismiss these feelings. However, they have not actually dismissed them; they have merely put them aside temporarily, to have them return at a later time. It is not easier later!

2. **When have I felt like this before?** What does this remind me of? The way you are feeling is not new. Take time to identify previous situations when you have experienced similar feelings, both in the recent past, and as a child. You will be able to identify repeating patterns of feelings and behaviours.

3. **What is the same; what is different?** We respond to what feels to be the same in this situation, as compared to previous situations. We need to balance it with what is different between these two situations. The 90:10 Rule reminds us that 90% of what you are feeling is not from the current situation. Put this aside for now, and deal with the Historian when the current situation is settled. Calmer, only a tenth of your initial reaction is all you need to help you deal with what you need to address now.

4. **What can I control about the current situation?** Generally, the main difference is that you now have more control than you felt as a child. You are not as helpless or powerless as you were. Identify what you can control, and focus on this.

This concept of the Personal Historian serves as the basis to optimize the benefits of different types of psychotherapy. Using a few psychotherapeutic approaches below as examples of this, I will show how this awareness can enhance your response to these treatments.

Ongoing Awareness of Your Personal Insecurities

Recognize that you, like other physicians, feel inadequate, and unconsciously enter all situations with this assumption, feeling that you have to try harder, just to get to where everyone else starts. Thus, you overachieve but are unaware of this.

This is what has helped you succeed to date, but to maintain this performance at each and every point is impossible and exhausting, and luckily, unnecessary. This awareness allows you to choose when and how much effort you will expend, and if you do choose to make a major effort, to at least give yourself credit for it.

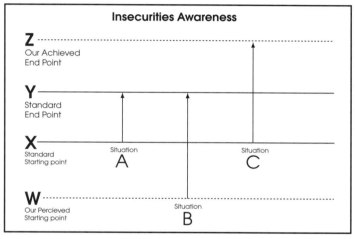

Diagram A – Starting from Behind

In the above diagram, the basic assumption (Situation A) is that other people start at Line X, and get to Line Y. However, as physicians, our Historian makes us feel that we start at a lower point at Line W, and so we have to work harder to get to Line Y (Situation B), where everyone else is. In reality, physicians start at Line X (Situation C), just like everyone else, and so the extra effort gets us to Line Z, a greater accomplishment. Thus, we can choose to attain Line Y, or any point between Lines Y and Z. If we do choose to get to Line Z, we can feel proud of our extra achievement.

Ongoing Awareness of Your Typical Response to Stress

As a child, in a particular situation, you learned to respond in a particular manner. This was effective; it got you through. However, it may not work as well in current situations. The good news is that you may not even need it now. As you begin to recognize this behaviour regularly, you can work to modify it.

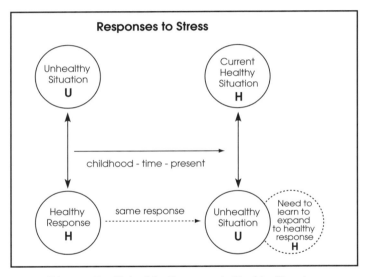

Diagram B – Unhealthy Responses in Healthy Situations

As a child in an unhealthy situation (U), you developed a response that was healthy and appropriate (H). Over time, you have maintained this same response. However, you are likely in a healthy situation now (H), and your old response is now unhealthy and unnecessary (U). You can learn to modify this response to become healthier (H).

Cognitive Therapy

The main goal of cognitive therapy is to help patients change maladaptive thinking and behaviours, and to learn healthier ways to behave. My goal is also to help you understand where you have learned this maladaptive thinking, so that you will maximally benefit from the cognitive therapy and recognize the "Historian" as the initial, ultimate cognitive distortion. Upon this basis, it is possible to recognize when we are thinking in this distorted manner, where it comes from and how it is not valid, and how to balance these distortions. Through cognitive therapy, you will see that how you think impacts on how you feel, and that negativity dominates when you feel depressed.

There are several types of cognitive distortions, as described by Dr. David Burns (1980). These include:

- All or nothing thinking: If you do not achieve perfection, then you feel you have failed.

- Overgeneralization: You view a single negative event as an ongoing pattern of failure.

- Mental filter: A single negative aspect becomes the focus and discolours your perception of the entire situation

- Disqualifying the positive: Anything positive you do is dismissed.

- Jumping to conclusions: You interpret situations and make negative conclusions and assumptions about yourself.

- Magnification or minimization: You exaggerate your errors and weaknesses, and underrate your successes and strengths.

- Emotional reasoning: You incorrectly feel that your emotions are based on reality.

- Should statements: You motivate yourself by what you feel you "should" do, causing guilt and frustration.

- Labeling: You label yourself inaccurately and negatively.

- Personalization: You take responsibility for negative events around you for which you are not responsible.

When you recognize these thoughts and consciously attribute them to the Historian, whom we now know is not accurate, then, you can best use cognitive therapy to challenge this thinking, and learn to improve your mood. We react to what is the same from our childhood experiences; we need to balance it with what is different in our current situation.

Child vs. Adult Exercise:

1. Take a sheet of paper to record your negative thoughts. Divide this paper into half lengthwise.

2 Draw a small child on the left-hand side of the page, and an adult on the right-hand side, both with "thought bubbles."

3. Write out your self-critical thoughts in the bubble on the left-hand side. This will make you consciously attribute these thoughts to the child, the Historian.

4. On the right-hand side, balance this with a more realistic evaluation of the situation you are in. This is your current adult perspective. It may help you to pretend that you are responding to a disclosure from an actual child you know and love, or your best friend— the "Best Friend" technique. It is initially easier for us to think more positively on the behalf of others instead of ourselves.

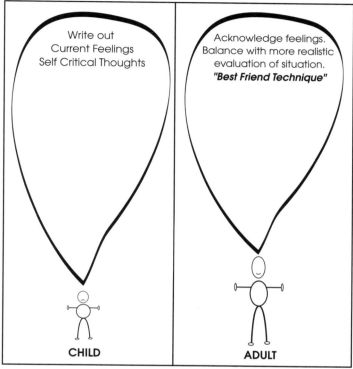

Write out
Current Feelings
Self Critical Thoughts

Acknowledge feelings.
Balance with more realistic
evaluation of situation.
"Best Friend Technique"

CHILD

ADULT

Diagram C – Child vs. Adult

Transactional Analysis

Dr. Eric Berne founded the theory of Transactional Analysis, highlighting that verbal communication is the basis of human social relationships. He stated that each person is made up of three ego states – parent, adult and child. Our feelings at the time determine which state we use, and we can shift from one state to another. Effective transactions, or communication, must be complementary, as crossed transactions cause upset and poor communication.

The healthiest interaction occurs as two adults interacting. In stressful situations we automatically assume roles that were assigned to us as children by the situation, and perpetuated by our personal Historian, and take on the child ego state. While we cannot change how others perceive us, we can identify and reassign ourselves new roles. Understanding that we took these roles on as children, we can identify when we unconsciously fall into them again, and learn to adopt adult roles more consistently. Even if others persist in taking on a parental, powerful role over us, we can remain as an adult. Over time, they will take on an adult role, too, to maintain a balanced relationship.

Teeter-Totter Exercise:

1. Imagine a teeter-totter in a playground. When two people are playing well, it is well-balanced and a lot of fun. This is what happens in an Adult-to-Adult relationship, the type that we want to cultivate and maintain.

2. Now, imagine that, thanks to our Historian, we feel insecure and inadequate in a situation, and react as a Child. Or, we can be with someone who is controlling and exerts power over us, as a parent could do to a child. We take on the Child role in response. Unfortunately, this is also balanced and can be maintained, but it is unhealthy. Recognize when you are in the Child role, and consciously resume the role of an Adult, and behave as such. This is the part that you control.

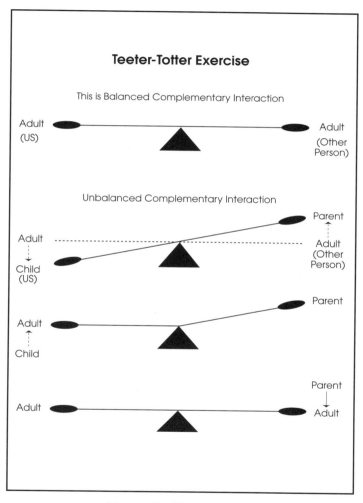

Diagram D – The Teeter-Totter

3. If the other person persists in the Parent role, the teeter-totter is off balance. Tolerate this temporary discomfort, as they try to "parent" an adult. Over time, in a viable relationship, they will drift to an Adult role.

DEALING WITH STRESS — SPECIALIZED DRILLS AND SKILLS

Twenty Training Tips

This chapter offers Twenty Training Tips; strategies that you can use immediately to better manage your stress. This is not rocket science. These strategies are probably the same things that you would advise for people you care about — family members, friends, colleagues, patients. Let's debunk the myth – Yes, you know about them, but you are not actually doing them yourself! Physician, heal thyself.

Imagine a cloud full of the names of these people you care about. Open that cloud slightly and add your name to it. Having understood why you could not allow yourself the same "luxury" in the past, let's consciously decide how you can move forward in a healthier way.

1. **Take care of yourself first.** When you initially board an airplane, and are taken through the safety demonstration, you are told, that in the event of an emergency, you must secure your own oxygen mask before you assist someone else. This is to ensure that you do not pass out before you can help others. You are no good to anyone else if you have passed out.

This is an excellent metaphor to use in your daily life. When you are in a stressful situation or feeling overloaded by demands, imagine yourself in a room with oxygen masks hanging down from the ceiling. Take time to do the metaphorical equivalent of putting your own mask on first. This means stopping to grab a sandwich on your way to see the patient in Emergency, or taking a moment to call your spouse at lunch to say hello. I know a colleague who can get through her whole day without stopping to go to the bathroom. Take the time to go; as far as I know, there is no award for holding it in!

We find it hard to take time for ourselves. We see this as being selfish, a luxury, something that we should not have to do. In fact, it is the opposite. It helps to see self-time as an investment. Investing time in ourselves allows us to be better available to meet the needs of others.

Essential ways to take care of ourselves include getting enough sleep, exercising regularly, ensuring good nutrition, and learning new things for interest.

Lack of sleep is the main complaint among physicians. Most adults require about 8 hours of sleep at night; less than half of us actually get this regularly. Try to get to bed a half hour earlier than usual. If you are going to stay up late, do fun things you want to do, not chores that you need to do. Sleep routines and rituals may help. Try getting to bed at the same time daily, and getting up at the same time each morning. Spend quiet time in your bedroom before falling asleep. Look for ways that you can achieve better sleep – limit your caffeine intake, limit alcohol use, do not exercise in the evening if it is too physically stimulating, minimize disruptions and distractions such as sounds and light. If you are thinking or worrying, write it down so you can put it away to deal with at another time.

Regular exercise is a natural and effective way to manage your stress, and remain healthy. Exercise not only produces endorphins that help you feel better, it also increases serotonin levels, just like antidepressants do. Don't wait until you feel you have more energy; exercise helps you create more energy and feel less fatigued.

Some physicians do not think their schedule allows them to commit to regular activity, but in fact, they are able to attend the majority of the scheduled sessions. Find ways to include activity into your daily routine – take the stairs, lift weights while watching television, bike to work. Find an activity that you enjoy. Work out with a friend. Be realistic, and don't try to do it perfectly. Do not defer it until you have done everything else you need to do. Make a commitment to it – yes, it's OK to be "selfish." Don't make it optional; put it in the same category as other things that you must do.

Proper nutrition is not always easy, but can help improve your ability to manage stress. Choose healthy foods in moderate quantities. Do not restrict yourself to the point where you feel deprived. Eat breakfast daily. Drink lots of water. Monitor your food-mood connection. If you eat when you are stressed, consciously choose to do something else such as walk, read, call a friend, or write in a journal. Have healthy snacks available. Try the Ten Rule: rate the taste out of ten, and only eat treats if they rate a full ten, and are worth it. Remember the Principle of

Diminishing Returns, which describes how the first treat is very special, the second one gives 80% of the satisfaction and enjoyment, and there continues to be a drop off in pleasure with each successive treat.

2. **Get your own family doctor.** Delegate your medical care to a colleague, and see him or her regularly. Less than half of all physicians have their own physician. Some of us cite lack of time to see a doctor. Sometimes, it is because there is no one available to take us on as patients. If you do not have a personal doctor, make it a project to obtain one as soon as you can.

   Many physicians who do have a family doctor have not seen him or her recently, or for regular checkups. These visits are saved for times when we are "really sick," since we don't want to be embarrassed by worrying about a small problem, or be seen as a complainer, or to bother them. Let yourself be a patient, and ask your family doctor to schedule regular appointments. Your job is just to show up for the appointment.

3. **Time Management**. With all the competing demands on our time, learning to manage time is an essential skill in medicine. If this is an area in which you struggle, it is worth investing in a good time management course.

   The key principle is organization, to avoid repetition and unnecessary work. Group similar activities, so you can do them all at the same time and be more efficient. For example, set aside a specific time daily to return phone calls, review lab results, or to phone in prescriptions. Handle every piece of paper only once – file it, toss it, or reply to it and fax back, or put it in an envelope and stamp it when you first look at it. Schedule activities and duties appropriately; do not over commit. Put aside specific time in your calendar to not just do the activity, but also plan and prepare for it. A note on my calendar reminds me "Warning! Dates on this calendar are closer than you think."

Another way to consider how to manage your time best is to consider everything that you do as being either Time-Creating (it takes time to do, but energizes you and leaves you feeling great or satisfied) or Time-Depleting (it takes time and is tedious, demanding, tiring, and not enjoyable). The same activity can be time-creating for one person, and time-depleting for another; and perhaps fit into one category at one point in your life, and into another at another point. Decide which of these two categories something falls into for you now, and spend more time doing things that create energy, and less time doing what drains you. It helps me to give up something that depletes me, when I know that this same activity, energizes others. I happily leave it for them to do.

One of the things I enjoy most is the time I spend with my group of medical students that I mentor. This group is young, excited, keen, and enthusiastic, and regularly reminds me of all the positive things that first drew me to medicine. I meet with them regularly, plan fun things to do, and make myself available to them as needed. Although, it takes a fair amount of time and energy, it is always so positive and nourishing for me. I would choose to meet with the mentor group one evening, over going to a meeting that I know would deplete me.

4. **Set Priorities**. We have so many pressing demands that we need to set priorities, and accept that we cannot do them all at the same time. What are all the things that I need to do? If I could only do one thing, what would that be? Repeat these questions, as required.

Most of us are very skilled at setting priorities for our work responsibilities – let's extrapolate this into our personal lives.

This is a skill that I gleaned from my husband, who learned it more easily and includes himself in his list of priorities. As an ER physician, when he works on the weekend, he has a couple of weekdays off. Ever since we were first married, he would ask me if there was anything I wanted him to do while he was off and I was at work, and suggest that I just leave him a list on the fridge. I would leave the list, and call home at lunchtime to see if he had completed it. That's what I would have done had someone left me a list — I would address it immediately, and then do what I wanted to do once it was completed. By lunchtime, he would have not even looked at the list. He had spent the morning doing things he wanted – exercising or doing some physical activity, and practicing his music. However, every afternoon, he would happily, easily, and efficiently deal with my list, feeling energized, and not resentful, because he had already met his own needs.

5. **Anticipate and prepare for situations**. If we know there are things we will be required to do, anticipating and preparing for them ensures that we feel some sense of control. Usually, we know this intellectually, but our drive to do as much as we

can makes us over commit and have less time to prepare for each event. This leads to our feeling rushed and stressed. This anticipation can help in all aspects of our life.

For example, at work, we cannot be in our office seeing patients at 3:00 pm, and be halfway across town at the medical school to teach the students at 3:00 pm. Anticipating the travel time saves a lot of stress.

At home, we found a great way to anticipate and save ourselves a lot of hassle. When the children were younger, one of our holidays each year was a trip without the children, which we eagerly anticipated. We would deal with any associated guilt in leaving the kids home, by bringing back gifts for them. However, we soon got tired of the process of shopping for the gifts, making room in the luggage for them, declaring them at customs. Instead, we anticipated the need for gifts, and before we left for our trip, we would go to Toys "R" Us, buy the gifts, wrap them and leave them in the garage at home to bring into the house upon our return!

6. **Consider and Use Options**. Knowing that we feel stress when we think that we do not have any choice or control, it helps to assume there is a choice and look for it. As we learned in medical school, you have to have a "high index of suspicion"; if you look for it, you are more likely to find it. Similarly, you have to adopt the following mantra. There is an option; what could it be?

There is no perfect solution, only solutions that work. Sometimes, we have to create our own solution. Enjoy it for as long as it lasts and works, then find another workable solution.

When our children were in grade school, we no longer had a full-time nanny at home. This worked fine for the most part, as we had great after-school care organized. The problem came when one of them was sick and could not go to school. I recall nights when I would hear one start to cough, and worry that he would not be well and could not go to school the next day. Since my husband could rarely find someone to cover his ER shifts at the last minute, it usually fell to me to cancel or rearrange my office. I would find this very stressful, torn between wanting to take care of both my family, and my patients. Then, I remembered there was a solution; I just had to find it.

I put an ad in the local community newspaper, and found a neighbour who was recently retired, who agreed to be "on call" for me, for a dollar a day. If I called her early in the morning, she would cancel her plans for the day and come into my home if I needed her to stay with a child who was feeling well enough that I did not feel I needed to be with him, but too sick to be at school.

7. **Learn to say NO**. We are capable, efficient, hard-working, conscientious and responsible. We do our best, people like our work, and so ask us to do more. We want to be nice, please others, and be liked. This makes it difficult for us to decline and say "No" to things that we are asked to do. But, as we are learning, we need to choose what we do and do not do, what our priorities are, and how to set aside time to care for ourselves.

There are some questions you can consider to decide if you will agree to the request. Ask yourself, "Do I want to do this?

Am I the only one who can do this? What will happen if I do not do this? What is in it for me?" If you do not want to do it, someone else could also do it, it is not a crisis situation, and there is little in it for you, consider saying No.

There are three easy steps to saying "No":
1. Open your mouth.

2. Say "No."

3. Close your mouth.

"No" is a complete sentence. The third step is the most difficult, as we want to continue and explain why we really cannot do it, how we would do it if we could, and keep explaining until we are absolved. Such a goal takes much effort, time and energy; and is usually unattainable. The good news is that if you do your share of the work and decline responsibly, others understand that you cannot be consistently available, and continue to value and respect you.

I was recently asked to submit the PowerPoint slides for a presentation a month away, with only two days' notice, as this would give time to have the slides translated into French. It was a Wednesday, and I was busy wrapping things up so I could get away on holidays that Friday. I had full days booked in the office, and had already set aside Wednesday and Thursday evening to deal with other things that I wanted to complete before I left. I briefly considered whether I could stay up even later than planned, and decided against that.

I replied that I was unable to submit the presentation slides by Friday as asked, and promised that I would attend to it the first Monday evening when I was back from holidays. The response was very positive, and they agreed and thanked me, telling me that this allowed them to schedule the translations, and they would get the other presentations translated first and wait for mine a week later.

8. **Add fun to work.** We choose to work. It can be more enjoyable than just a job if we consciously look for ways to add fun to the process. This can take the form of a Journal Club, an annual golf day, barbecues, annual parties with family included, or active retreats with colleagues in which you do things that you would not otherwise do together (rock climbing, laser tag, mountain biking). Take fun seriously. Fun is the verb of joy, and helps you focus in the present.

Slow down and enjoy what you can in the moment. As my colleague in the office says, "Don't rush life. You're dead for a very long time."

A healthy work environment is a major determinant of our own health, and is enhanced by a sense of teamwork, and shared positive experiences. It allows us to get to know other aspects of the people we work with, and be known by our colleagues, in an appropriately more personal manner. This helps us to identify people at work who have similar challenges balancing their lives (young children, finding a housekeeper, aging parents), and obtain their advice and support.

Meeting colleagues in a fun environment enables us to start, and maintain, an Emotional Bank Account with them. This is a concept that encourages the building of a virtual account between two people, in which you can bank positive emotions – get to know them as people, find out what they like, what they do, what is important to them; and then ask them about it when you can, building positive connections. If every one at work opened up such an account with every one else they worked with, and made regular deposits, then the one day someone is stressed and irritable, they can make a withdrawal, yet still have plenty in the bank to spare. This allows us to communicate better, build mutual trust, have fewer misperceptions, resolve conflicts more easily, and express appreciation of each other regularly.

9. **Plan for transition times**. Moving between our work and personal environment is not always easy or smooth. This makes it difficult to leave behind one set of responsibilities, and fully enjoy the next. Planning for these transitions helps to minimize the stress involved.

Stop before you start. Take a few minutes at the end of your day, and consciously consider what is ahead and waiting for you at the next point. Mentally put yourself into that situation, so you can ease into it, and be ready for it. Some colleagues take a few minutes to reflect on this before they leave the office at the end of the work day, some take time on the drive home to think about it, some bike or walk home and reenergize themselves, others phone home before leaving to see what is happening and what they can do to help.

When you get home, seek people out and say hello.

This transition time is useful when moving from work to home, but also plan for this at the start of the day when going from home to work. It does help the day go better, if we give ourselves some time to get started each morning.

Also, another time where a planned transition works well is just before or after a vacation. Anticipate the extra work you may need to complete before you leave; or the phone calls, emails and lab results that have piled up in your absence. Plan when and where you will do this. Some physicians plan to keep some time clear from clinical work, to attend to this.

I recognized the need for a conscious time to make the transition when I arrived home from a busy day at the office, to my three sons, then aged two, two, and three years. I came into the house, reached down to untie my shoes, and the three of them rounded the corner and hurled themselves at me, eager to see me and give me a hug. In their enthusiasm, they knocked me over, and my head went back and hit the wall behind me. My initial reaction was to be angry with them, and admonish them to be more careful. I immediately recognized how this was really my issue, that in fact, I would have more reason to be upset if they did not care if I were home, and ignored me. I began to anticipate coming home to them, and their exuberance, with great enjoyment.

10. **Don't take your work home**. Yes, I know this is easier said than done. However, I believe this is a rule we need to set for ourselves. Then, if we break it, it becomes the

exception to the rule, and not the new reality. There are many responsibilities in our work as physicians, and we do not always get them completed by the end of our workday. Our first line of action needs to be to reassess all that we are doing at work, and see what we can give up to create time for this project, not just assume that the time we will give up comes from our family and personal time.

If we do decide that this is the exception, then we must address this effectively. Even though we are used to making decisions and taking control, this is not the time or place to do this. This is still true, even if we know we have made the best decision; it was simply not ours to make alone. We need to respect and appreciate the people we live with. We cannot go home and tell our family when we have decided we will be working and be unavailable. We need to go home and find out what everyone else was hoping to do and when, let him or her know that we would like some time for this project, and ask what might be a good time. If this impacts your family, they need to be a part of the decision- making process. Also, if they helped to come up with the solution, they will not be resentful, and be happier and more supportive in your work.

Once you reach a mutually agreeable plan, do your part and stick to it. Start when you said that you were going to start, and stop when you said you would stop. Your work will still be there when you get back to it. You want to make sure the same is true of your family. When you are with your family, put your work away and give them your undivided attention. They deserve it.

I needed a few hours to work on a presentation during the weekend. Knowing my family's schedule, and trying to meet everyone's needs, I figured that I would have enough time to do it on Saturday morning if my husband took the kids to their swimming lessons, and had his own workout at the same time. However, it was not up to me to plan this for everyone. I told my family that I needed a couple of hours over the weekend to work, and asked what their plans were and how they thought it might work best. My husband offered to take the boys to their swimming lessons, was pleased that he could fit in a workout without intruding on family plans, and gave me the time I needed.

11. **Take regular time off**.   Everyone needs a holiday, a time to get away from work, to relax, and to meet their own needs. I know that many physicians do not take regular time off. There are a variety of reasons for this. We have too much work to do, and find it hard to get away. We put it off until something gets done, but then something new comes up to take its place. We cannot find someone to cover our practice while we are away. We need to work to meet our financial commitments.   While we can rationalize deferring the vacation, this deferral always takes its toll.

We need to take regular time off – a few minutes daily, an hour, a half-day, a full day, a week or longer. Plan these in advance, and see them as a crucial investment that allows you to meet all your commitments.

Use the Tarzan Rule, explained to me by Dr. Alan Buchanan, of Vancouver. Like Tarzan, who swings through the jungle letting go of one vine only after he has the other one in hand, do not end a holiday without having the next one planned.

While our schedules do not allow us to plan regular time off, waiting for our schedules to clear and making it happen often becomes an infinite wait. When we use the Tarzan Rule with all the events in our life that help us feel good, it ensures that we continue to experience the things that are positive for us.

Even if you do manage to get away for a holiday, it takes just a few days to dim the calming after-effects; and after about three weeks, the stress levels are back up. Take a mini-vacation daily – visualize your favourite holiday spot, meditate at your desk, take a stroll at lunch.

Sometimes, we have time off that we did not plan, such as when we are stuck in a traffic jam, when we choose the slowest line-up at the grocery store, or when a patient is late for an appointment. We can either allow ourselves to get upset and stressed in these situations, or find the positive benefits of this extra time. These are the Gifts of Time which Dr. Philip Burnard describes; plan for them, look for them, and appreciate them.

When I am caught in a traffic jam, and know that I am running late, I have to remind myself that looking at my watch more often will not get me there any faster. Instead, I reach for my favourite CD, and listen to music that I love but rarely listen to since the children's music has somehow invaded my car. I arrive at my destination, still a few minutes late, but feeling restored instead of stressed.

12. **Use support systems**. Look around you and identify resources that are available to you, to improve and maintain your health. These resources include people, programs and organizations. A current listing of some of these resources is at the back of this book.

Reach out to people you know. Ask questions of your colleagues when needed, and do not worry about seeming "too stupid" – that is just the Historian, and more likely, you will hear a response that confirms that is a good question and one that they have asked in the past, and find a colleague who is happy to help.

Seek mentors, people who have more experience than you in specific areas, and ask them to help you. They are invaluable resources. You do not have to be monogamous; you can have more than one mentor. While there are some formal mentor programs, you can find one yourself. Look for someone who is doing what you would like to be doing, and seems to be happy doing it, and go and introduce yourself to them. Do not be put off by your assumptions that they are too busy or don't want to be bothered by you – they are busy, but are happy to share their experience and see you progress.

Find people at work and at home, for whom you do not have to pretend to be anything different, with whom you feel comfortable and can just be yourself. Make time to make friends and to nurture these friendships. Recent research by Laura Klein at UCLA, shows that friends are especially important for women to reduce stress. Under stress, women produce a cascade of neurochemical hormones, including oxytocin and estrogen, which leads to bonding, which lessens the stress and produces a calming effect. Friends make the difference between a lonely and a lively life. They nurture, protect, support and listen to us. Medicine makes it hard for us to make and maintain friends; use the Tarzan Rule to maintain these connections.

If friends are unavailable, join a club that centres on an activity that you enjoy – a sport, a skill such as cooking or wine tasting, a film or book club, to meet with people and do things you like doing. Pets are a great source of support, providing companionship on demand, and unconditional love.

13. **Share your stories**. Sometimes, even when surrounded by caring people, we find it hard to open up and acknowledge the situation in which we feel stress. The "S" words go together; Secrets lead to Shame, while Sharing leads to Support. If we keep something a secret, it becomes associated with a sense of shame. You are in good company. Share your story with someone you trust, and you will receive support at the very time that you need it. In fact, you will realize that you are not alone, that other people whom you like and respect have experienced the same thing. This helps to normalize your situation, show that stress is inherent in medicine, and fill you with a sense of hope and resolution.

I was devastated when our nanny decided to leave, upon hearing that I was expecting twins. I worried about how I would find reliable and caring childcare, for three young babies. As I articulated my concerns after a departmental meeting ended, I was pleased to receive several suggestions on how to find childcare that other colleagues had used successfully.

14. **Remember the 90:10 Rule**. In any situation in which you feel stress and think that you are overreacting, you probably are. Remember, 90% of your reaction is from the past, the Historian. Only 10% of your reaction is due to the situation you are currently dealing with. Recognize and untwist the cognitive distortions that lead you to doubt yourself, and gain confidence.

Such reframing of the situation allows you to calm yourself down to a tenth of your initial response, and helps you to better deal with the situation. Reframing is a useful tool in many situations that cause us stress. Sometimes, it can provide immediate relief.

I became frustrated last year when my children began to play musical instruments at school. They would practice in the living room, and leave their musical instruments lying on the sofas, and their sheet music all over the coffee table. The room began to fill up, with an upright bass, three guitars and an amplifier, a set of drums and bongos, a piano, a trumpet and a flugelhorn, music stands…I would come home from work, and pick up sheet music before I took my coat off. This was not how I was raised to maintain my living room. What if company ever dropped by unexpectedly? Then, one day, I decided that we no longer had a living room, but a music room instead. (We rarely used it anyway, and all company – expected or otherwise – seemed to prefer the kitchen.) In the newly reframed music room, it is now entirely permissible to use and leave instruments and music accessible.

15. **Set realistic expectations**. Acknowledge your need to please others, and to be perfect. As you start to recognize the cognitive distortions you have perpetuated, and let them go, you can begin to have more realistic expectations of yourself. Good enough is really good enough. It becomes easier to do what is necessary, be more efficient, and not put off things because we thought it would take too long to do it properly. This allows us to write shorter, but more concise notes in

patients' charts, not vacuum the house every time before company comes, allow ourselves to get take-out if we are entertaining the day after call. We succeed more consistently, with less effort. We are better able to delegate, and set healthier limits for ourselves. When we achieve more than is required, we can give ourselves credit for that. We do not set ourselves up to fail. It is helpful to set similar realistic expectations of our family and friends too, and allows these relationships to be more relaxed and healthier.

As soon as we would get a whiff of what the children were able to do, we would want them to do it properly and perfectly, often before they were totally ready. I remember trying to walk to the park when they first learned to walk, fighting the crowds to skate on the Canal when they first learned to skate, and planning a family holiday to Prince Edward Island as they were learning to swim. This holiday helped us come up with our Holiday Rule, to assist in setting more realistic expectations. The rule is that when we decide what holiday we want to do with the children, we wait and do it the following year!

16. **Learn a relaxation technique**. This is a great skill to have. There are many different types of relaxation methods – passive, active, breathing techniques, yoga, tai-chi, meditation and spiritual relaxation.

I can promise guaranteed results with any of these, with one stipulation – that you choose one and practice it regularly. The practice is the key to success with such a technique. My husband plays in the Symphony, and when he gets the music for the upcoming concert, he practices, goes to the rehearsals, and goes over difficult parts of it over and over until he perfects it. The evening of the performance, when he is on stage with the Symphony, he just eases into it effortlessly. The time that you are experiencing stress is the performance; it is too late then to practice the relaxation technique. Pick one you feel will help you, and practice it over and over again when you are feeling calm, so it will be available for you to ease into when required.

Here is a good relaxation technique to try, which is a combination of several different methods, takes only five minutes to do, can be done almost anywhere, and requires no special equipment.

Find a quiet spot, and settle into a comfortable position. Close your eyes. Take a long, slow breath in, breathing through your nose, filling up your lungs, and hold it ever so slightly; then, very slowly let it all out. Do this again a second time. Then, resume your normal breathing, in a relaxed manner.

Let your mind drift away, to a relaxing spot... You are on a dune, overlooking a quiet secluded cove with a beautiful sandy beach that stretches forever. This is your own special place. No one else knows about it or can intrude. You can come any time you wish. To your right, there are some steps leading down to the beach. Let's take them down — 1-2-3-4-5-6-7-8-9-10.

You are now on the beach. Take off your socks and shoes. Wriggle your toes in the sand. You can feel each grain of sand under your feet. As you walk toward the water, you feel the grains of sand become cooler and more tightly packed. Then, you reach the sea, and a small wave laps around your ankles, cooling you off. You walk along the water's edge, enjoying the touch of the warm sun overhead, the sounds of the birds in the distance, and the trees softly swaying in the light breeze, the smell of the ocean, the gentle waves that cool your ankles.

You see a hammock slung between a couple of trees, and walk towards it. Ease yourself into the hammock, and lie back comfortably. Imagine a point in the middle of your forehead, from which will come a wave of relaxation. Focus on this point, as it starts a sense of relaxation. It widens to become a circle, and then covers your entire forehead, easing out any frowns and wrinkles, leaving it smooth and relaxed. This wave of relaxation moves back over your scalp, massaging it, lapping back and forth over any point where you may feel a headache until it is eased, leaving your scalp refreshed and tingly. The wave continues down over the back of your neck, massaging the muscles on either side of your spine. Your head feels heavy; let it drop gently to one side if it feels right. The wave continues over your shoulders, massaging and easing out the tension and knots. It continues into your arms, making your upper arms and your lower arms warm and heavy, and then moves into your hands and fingers. As the wave goes out of your body through the tips of each finger, imagine it taking out all of the stress of your upper body with it.

The wave continues down from your forehead, over your face, smoothing your face, leaving the skin silky. It goes over your eyelids, leaving them heavy and relaxed. It continues over your jaw, loosening it slightly, preventing your clenching, into your neck. The wave moves over your chest, easing your breathing, calming it, making it slow, regular, rhythmic.

The wave continues down your back, massaging all the muscles on either side of your spine, finding and easing out the knots, leaving you relaxed. It's almost like you're floating in the hammock. Enjoy this feeling. You can have it anytime you want. Even counting from 1 to 10 will help you get this feeling. You can associate this feeling with the word "ten," to use if you need to calm down quickly.

Then the wave moves on into your legs, making them feel heavy and warm. As the wave goes into your feet, imagine it moving back and forth slowly, massaging the muscles you have walked on all day,

As the wave goes out of your body through the tips of your toes, imagine it taking all the stress and tension out with it, leaving you feeling relaxed and calm. Enjoy this feeling for a few minutes.

Slowly, gradually, ease yourself up from the hammock. Make your way back to the steps. Let's count up the steps 10-9-8-7-6-5-4-3-2-1. Anytime after we get to 1, slowly open your eyes, and leave your body relaxed and your mind refreshed and energized to get on with the rest of your day.

Spirituality has been demonstrated to bring about healing. It is felt that religious commitment enhances health, and evidence shows that prayer can play a therapeutic role in physical and mental disease.

While spirituality overlaps with religion, it does not need to be confined within the structure of any specific set of religious beliefs. It defines how we feel about ourselves and our world. It offers a sense of meaning and purpose to our life, and provides inspiration that assists us in healing our stress. Believing in a higher power allows us to put our stress in perspective. The part of the situation over which we have no control, can be left to this higher power to worry about. It also allows us to believe that there may be a reason for these stresses, thereby providing a positive aspect of the problems.

17. **Laugh more often**. Laughter has been proven to have therapeutic benefits. Dr. Lee Berk and his associates at Loma Linda University have studied the effects of laughter on the immune system, and shown that laughter lowers blood pressure, reduces stress hormones, increases muscle flexion and boosts immune function. Laughter helps to reduce stress and elevate mood.

Children naturally use this, and laugh about 500 times a day. By the time we reach adulthood, it has decreased to 5-15 times a day. Striving to find humour in your day, and laugh at situations rather than complain will improve your mood, and the mood of those around you. Your ability to laugh at yourself and your situations will help in reducing your level of stress and make life more fun and enjoyable. Laughing is contagious, and helps you to connect to people around you.

Surround yourself with humour. Look for it regularly, and share it with your family, friends and colleagues. Our waiting room has several humour anthologies. Watch funny television sitcoms, movies or plays. Read humorous books and cartoons, or the comics in the daily newspaper. A friend of mine sends me a daily laugh via email.

18. **Take solo time**. Take time for your self, to be alone. Find a space where you do not have to be responsible for anyone or anything. Ask for this solitude, and use the Tarzan Rule to keep it happening. Offer the same to your partner. Time alone is on the same continuum of intimacy as time together, and is an essential part of a healthy relationship. Openly acknowledge and address the associated sense of being selfish. Consider this time alone as an investment in all the relationships in your life — with your partner, children, friends, community and patients.

19. **Plan your finances**. This is the second most common reason why physicians do not do the things they need to do, to better manage their stress. They do not feel that they have the money to do things, such as take a holiday, take a time management course, or learn to mountain bike. They have major financial commitments, and feel they need to work constantly to reduce their debt as soon as they can.

The reality is that they cannot afford not to take a break. Such overwork will lead to burnout, and force time off – without any planning, preparation or enjoyment. Physicians are known to be poor money managers, and do not have the training or expertise to do this. Some handle their money by the "Christopher Columbus" method, where, financially, they do not know where they are going, and do not know where they are when they get there.

Learn to manage your finances. Stick to the basic principles. Have a clear financial goal; pay your non-deductible debts off first; institute a regular savings plan with pre-authorized payments; do not overextend and live outside your means; implement your plan and reassess regularly.

There are many resources to help you in financial planning and management. Some physicians avoid these resources, as they feel that they do not have time to seek their advice, or feel embarrassed that they cannot do this on their own, or feel ashamed that they have poorly managed their finances to date and will be "found out." They are experts and want to help. Make use of them, so you can financially plan regular holidays, pace yourself better at work, work consistently, and be able to retire when you would like.

20. **Let go of the guilt**. Guilt is the most common reason why we do not make the changes we need to, to remain healthy. We do not take holidays, or leave work on time, or take an evening off, because we feel guilty. Guilt prevents us from doing something just for ourselves, which we did not have to do, after which there is nothing tangible to show for it. Guilt is a feeling that we experience when we feel we have not met others' expectations. Knowing that these expectations were inaccurate assumptions, based on our Historian, we can learn to reassess this, and see that we are, indeed meeting, and often surpassing expectations.

There is no need for the guilt. We are highly responsible people, and have such a sensitive inbuilt system of censorship.

Any thought that is wrong, illegal, unethical, immoral, unreasonable or irresponsible is already censored out. Thus, if a thought makes it to our consciousness, it is because it is acceptable. How do we deal with our guilt? First, we acknowledge that we feel guilty; and then we let it go, knowing that it is unnecessary. A rule of thumb about guilt is that if you are thinking of doing something that makes you feel guilty, that is the very thing that you should do!

I felt enormous guilt as I considered changing my office hours to reduce my stress, as it would allow me to finish my work earlier each day and be home with the children after school, to spend more time with them, to help with homework, and plan healthier meals.

The guilt was a result of the impact on my patients, as it would require some of them to change the timing of their regular appointments. However, I followed through with the plans, only because I had promised the children that I would make this change.

None of my patients was angry, the appointments were rescheduled, and several of them appreciated the role modeling and made similar changes in their work schedules. The children were happy to have me at home. Evenings were so much easier, with the homework done before dinner, dinners planned and prepared, and more time for scheduled or family activities. My level of stress was markedly reduced. What I was contemplating doing, but made me feel guilty, was the very thing I needed to do.

In summary, the Twenty Training Tips work well. Use them regularly. Focus on one that is of particular need or interest, and use it in interval training. Mix the tips up for a personalized cross-training experience. This is the race of your life. Stay fit, and enjoy!

CHAPTER 9

MAINTAINING STRENGTH AND ENDURANCE

Yeah, this all sounds great! But, how do I actually incorporate this into my daily life?

This is the most commonly asked question at the end of the many presentations that I give to my colleagues.

Change is Stressful

Change is never easy — to make, or to maintain. As physicians, even when we want to make a change and improve our level of stress, it is not an easy process. Change itself is stressful. We try to make too many changes all at once. We make changes that do not need to occur, and do not limit changes to only the necessary ones. We expect change to happen quickly.

Barriers to Change

There are several barriers to change. We are stuck in our habits, and find it easy to maintain the way we are used to doing things. There is a behavioural law of inertia, which reinforces the habits and resists the change. Sometimes, we fear the change, as it is the unknown, and we sense a lack of control over the outcome. There is inherent performance anxiety, as we are unsure what will be required of us, and if we are able to perform to expectations. Physicians prefer to stick to things that we know we can do well. Other barriers to change are assumptions about lack of necessary resources – the time, energy or money to make the change. Since these are assumptions, we must check them out and see if we can bypass this barrier.

It helps to remember why we wanted to make the change. Usually, we make a change for one set of reasons, but then lose sight of this and unfairly assess it based on another set of parameters and find it wanting.

When I decided to reduce my time in the office to decrease my stress in meeting the needs of my family, I looked at the first decrease in income and wondered if I had done the right thing. I had to remember my initial goals, review the positive impact of lessening the stress, and was able to conclude that I had made a good change.

Change-Back Messages

Watch out for "Change-Back Messages." Sometimes, making the change feels absolutely right to us. However, soon after, we are tested by others, who may have supported the change in theory, but actually preferred you the way you were and now want you to change back. Sometimes, these messages are overt, sometimes they are more subtle. Look out for them, recognize them as they happen, and call them what they are. The best way to handle a Change-Back Message is to resist it. Do not change back. Allow people to express their concerns, reassure them; and continue doing as you have planned, and give them time to see that this change is good.

Stages of Change

There are several stages of making a change. Prochaska and associates (1992) described a similar process. These include:

1. Pre-Contemplation: There is an awareness of the need for a change.

2. Contemplation: Identifying your choices, and making a specific decision to change. Ensure that you set realistic goals.

3. Preparation: Resolving to make a commitment to the change.

4. Action: Set a plan of action towards the change.

5. Maintenance: Regular reassessment and evaluation.

Pre-Contemplation

The very fact that you are reading this book is proof of your awareness of the need to make some changes to improve your level of stress as a physician.

Contemplation

The bulk of this book has been devoted to helping you realize that you have choices, identifying choices available to you, and helping you make decisions toward change.

Preparation

Set a goal that represents what you want to achieve. Then, break it down into a series of smaller steps that are tangible and allow you to succeed. Make sure that you set goals that are **SMART**—Specific, Measurable, Achievable, Relevant and Timely. Although this is described in their book *High Performance*

Racing, Merricks' and Walker's winning approach to goal setting is applicable to any ambition.

The commitment must come from you. Resolve that you must change, that it must happen now, and that you can deal with the process of change. If you do not aim for it, you cannot reach it. This is not easy to do, so allow yourself some time and latitude in doing it. I tell patients that they have to hear something 18 times before it sinks in. This is an arbitrary number, but signifies that once is not enough, not even twice, five times, ten times, or even fifteen times. You have to hear it, consider it and integrate it over and over. In my office, I am very prepared to repeat as needed. Leave this book where you can pick it up as often as needed, during this process.

Action

So, how do you move forward toward action? Don't just try! Humour me as I help you see what this means. While you are reading, please stand up. There, you've done it. Now, sit back down again. This time, I will ask you, not to stand up, but to try to stand up. See, this time it is different; most of us do not actually achieve the end result of standing. This serves to illustrate the difference between doing something, and trying to do something. Decide what specific strategy you will use, and make specific steps to implement it. Don't just try.

It also helps to set a specific date for the change, and openly make an agreement with others, tell them what you are planning to do (especially if it is of benefit to them!), and they will help to prod you towards action.

When I considered working shorter days in the office to spend more time with my children, I was aware of my guilt holding me back, and told the children that I would be able to pick them up after school in September of the next year. Having promised them, and seeing them eagerly anticipate this all summer, helped propel me to action.

Maintenance

How do you maintain positive change in the long term? Do not expect this to be an immediate and permanent change. It is very easy to slip back into old patterns. We are only humans — and very caring, conscientious and responsible ones, at that.

Expect that you will slip and that this is normal. Plan to catch yourself before it goes on for too long, and get back on track. The standard progress through this process is a spiral one.

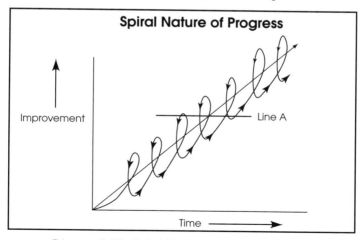

Diagram E. The Spiral Nature of Progress in Therapy

Over time, we expect to maintain a steady linear improvement. In fact, this is not what really happens. We do progress forward, but in a spiral fashion. There are highs, always followed by lows. The lows always feel as difficult as they were in the past. However, remember that the lows occur less frequently over time, and take less time and energy to resolve. Each low is not as low as the preceding one. In fact, as line A shows, over time, the bottom of the low is where the top of the high used to be!

Use "Birthday Reminders" to help you. Use the date of your birthday each year as an opportunity to remind yourself to stop and assess where you are, on an annual basis. Put time aside on that date, and take stock of how you feel about all aspects of your life – your relationship with your partner, children, friends, neighbours; your work and sense of satisfaction with the focus of work, the results, the money you earn; time and attention to the home and the house; vacations you have taken; time for yourself and your attention to your level of exercise, nutrition and sleep. This is a good time to set new goals or to reset old ones.

Then, each month on that date, plan to set aside time and review the same things. This allows you to catch that you are not on track within a few weeks, and quickly make the adjustments required. Before you finish the review each month, use the Tarzan Rule to make sure that you have put time aside a month later to follow up.

This is an ongoing process. We all chose medicine for a reason; it is rewarding and fulfilling. It is worth making the effort to ensure that this career continues to be a satisfying one.

APPENDIX

BOOKS SPECIFIC TO PHYSICIAN HEALTH

Burnard P. *Coping with Stress in the Health Professions: A Practical Guide*. London: Chapman and Hall; 1991.

Gabbard G, Menninger R. *Medical Marriage*. Washington, DC: APA Press; 1988.

Goldman LS, Myers M, Dickstein LJ. *The Handbook of Physician Health*. Chicago: AMA Press; 2000.

Grainger C. *Stress Survival Guide*. London: BMJ Publishing Group; 1994.

Myers MF. ed. *CMA Guide to Physician Health and Well-being: facts, advice, and resources for Canadian doctors*. Ottawa: Canadian Medical Association; 2003.

Myers MF. *Doctors' Marriages: A Look at the Problems and Their Solutions*. 2nd ed. New York: Plenum Publishing; 1998.

Nace EP. *Achievement and Addiction: A Guide to the Treatment of Professionals*. New York: Brunner/Mazel; 1995.

Peterkin AD. *Staying Human During Residency Training*. Ottawa: Canadian Medical Association; 1991.

Sotile WM, Sotile MO. *The Medical Marriage: A Couples Survival Guide*. New York: Carol Publishing; 1995.

Sotile WM, Sotile MO. *Beat Stress Together*. New York: John Wiley and Sons, Inc.; 1998.

Sotile WM, Sotile MO. *The Resilient Physician: Effective Emotional Management for Doctors and their Medical Organizations*. Chicago: AMA Press; 2002.

GENERAL BOOKS

Berne E. *Games People Play: The Psychology of Human Relationships*. New York: Ballantine Books; 1964.

Burns D. *Feeling Good: The New Mood Therapy*. New York: William Morrow and Co.; 1980.

Collins J. *Good To Great*. New York: HarperCollins Publishers Ltd.; 2001.

Davis M, Eshelman ER, McKay M. *The Relaxation and Stress Reduction Workbook*. Oakland CA: New Harbinger Publications; 1982.

Elkin A. *Stress Management for Dummies*. Foster City CA: IDG Books worldwide, Inc.; 1999.

Greenberger D, Padesky C. *Mind Over Mood: Changing How You Feel By Changing The Way You Think*. New York: Guilford Publications; 1995.

Maslach C, Leither MP. *The Truth About Burnout*. San Francisco: Josey-Bass Publishers; 1997.

Merricks J, Walker I. *High Performance Racing*. Great Britain: Fernhurst Books 1996.

Stewart I, Joines V. *TA Today: A New Introduction to Transactional Analysis*. Chapel Hill NC: Lifespace Publishing; 1987.

REFERENCE ARTICLES

Berk LS, Felton DL, Tan SA, Bittman BB, Westengard J. Modulation of Neuroimmune Parameters During the Eustress of Humor-Associated Mirthful Laughter. *Alternative Therapies in Health* March 2001; 7(2)

Prochaska JO, DiClemente CC, Norcross JC. In search of how people change: applications to addictive behaviors. *Am Psychol* 1992; 47:1102-14.

Taylor SE, Klein LC, Lewis BP, Gruenewald TL, Gurung RAR, Updegraff JA. Female Response to Stress: Tend and Befriend, Not Fight or Flight. *Psychological Review* 2000; 107(3): 41-429.

Western Journal of Medicine. Jan. 2001 – entire issue is devoted to Physician Health.

Member's Dialogue. Jul.-Aug. 2003. This issue of this publication of the College of Physicians and Surgeons of Ontario (CPSO) focuses on Physician Health.

Virtual Mentor. Sept. 2003. This on-line journal of the American Medical Association devoted this issue to Physician Health.

Stress Management For Busy Professionals. Boulder, CO: CareerTrack, Inc.; 1991.

CMA Physician Resource Questionnaire. Ottawa: Canadian Medical Association; 2003.

RESOURCES

Canada

Canadian Medical Association Centre for Physician Health and Well-being
www.cma.ca

The Canadian Physician Health Network (CPHN) – alliance of provincial and territorial physician health programs:

- Prince Edward Island: 1-888-368-7303 www.mspei.pe.ca

- Newfoundland and Labrador: 1-800-563-9133

- New Brunswick: 1-506-458-8860 www.nbms.nb.ca

- Nova Scotia: 1-902-468-8215

- Quebec: 1-514-397-0888 www.qphp.org

- Ontario: 1-800-851-6606 www.phpoma.org

- Manitoba: 1-204-237-8320

- Saskatchewan (and Northwest Territories): 1-306-244-2196 www.sma.sk.ca

- Alberta (and Yukon): 1-877-767-4637 www.albertadoctors.org

- British Columbia: 1-604-742-0747 www.physiciansupportprogram.ca

United States

Federation of State Physician Health Programs (FSPHP) – United States national umbrella organization for the individual state physician health programs. Contact AMA Physician Health Program at 312-464-5066.

NOTES:

NOTES: